ECOLOGY GREEN PAGES

FOR
STUDENTS AND TEACHERS

from
The KIDS' STUFF™ People

Incentive Publications, Inc.
Nashville, Tennessee

Special acknowledgement is accorded to:

Kathy LaMorte and Sharen Lewis for compiling and organizing the materials included in this publication.

Susan Harrison for the cover illustration.

Jan Keeling, editor.

Library of Congress Catalog Card Number: 92-74237
ISBN 0-86530-269-3

TABLE OF CONTENTS

DID YOU KNOW?

Fast Facts

- Paper = 39% of our waste; yard trash = 15%; food waste = 10%; plastic = 9%; wood, glass, metals, and others account for the rest.

- The current worldwide carbon dioxide releases from burning fossil fuels alone totals 22 billion tons per year.

- Burning one gallon of gasoline produces two pounds of carbon dioxide.

- Using one kilowatt-hour of electricity from a coal-powered plant produces two pounds of carbon dioxide.

- Flying one mile in an airplane generates a half-pound of carbon dioxide per passenger per mile.

- The average per capita production of carbon dioxide in North America is five tons per year.

- Current computer models predict that the average global temperature may rise by several degrees Fahrenheit within the next century if global warming is not checked. By comparison, world temperatures rose just one degree in the past 100 years.

- There are presently (1990 Census) almost 6 billion people on the Earth. That figure is expected to double in 60 years.

- Americans use about 600 pounds of paper per person per year, but less than 30% is recycled. Recycling saves natural resources (energy, trees, water) and reduces air and water pollution.

- Making recycled paper uses 61% less water and produces 70% fewer pollutants than making paper from virgin fibers. 33% fewer energy resources are used in the production of recycled paper than in the production of new paper. Recycling a ton of newsprint is equal to saving 168 gallons of oil.

- Recycling a three-foot stack of newspapers saves one tree. Recycling one ton of newspapers saves 17 trees.

- Paper products contribute to 39% of our solid waste. 85% of the waste produced in schools is paper.

- Publishing the Sunday edition of the *NEW YORK TIMES* consumes 10,000 trees each week.

- According to the EPA, the U.S. will bury or burn the following material in the year 2000: 11.4 million tons of newsprint, 16.2 million tons of corrugated cardboard, 10.8 million tons of glass packaging, 8.2 million tons of plastic packaging, and 1.5 million tons of aluminum packaging. If those 48.1 million tons were recycled instead, the equivalent of 10.1 billion gallons of gasoline

DID YOU KNOW? *(cont.)*

Fast Facts

would be saved. That is enough gasoline to power 15.4 million cars for one year (assuming 18.3 mpg and 12,000 miles per year for each car). In addition, recycling would result in reduced water use and reduced water and air pollution.

• A large coal-fired plant can emit in a single year as much sulfur dioxide as was blown out by the 1980 eruption of Mt. Saint Helens—some 400,000 tons.

• In Brazil alone, an area the size of Nebraska—76,000 sq. mi.—of rain forest is destroyed each year.

• Rain forests account for only 7% of the Earth's land surface but contain 50% of the Earth's trees and more than 10 million species of plants and animals.

• Each year the Earth's population increases by 85 million people.

• The U.S. churns out more than 432,000 tons of garbage daily.

• Japan recycles 95% of its newspaper, 55% of its steel, 66% of its bottles, and 40% of its aluminum.

• In just one year America buries enough metals to build two million cars and enough wood to construct one million homes.

• The U.S. imports $2.2 billion worth of rain forest hardwood per year.

• 45 million chopsticks made from rain forest hardwoods are imported by Japan every month.

• Every second an acre of tropical rain forest is destroyed.

• In the U.S. more than 7.6 million television sets, each loaded with recyclable materials, are thrown out every year.

• In one year the U.S. dumps enough aluminum to build 500,000 mobile homes.

• It costs $20 billion a year to process our garbage.

• Styrofoam takes thousands of years to decompose, yet the U.S. makes 25 billion styrofoam containers each year, most of which end up in landfills.

• Around the world hundreds of millions of pounds of hazardous waste are produced each year.

• Nineteen trillion gallons of waste are dumped directly into the oceans each year. That's almost 2,000 times the amount dumped in the *Exxon Valdez* oil accident.

• Despite the 1972 Clean Water Act, factories and cities in the U.S. continue to dump about 5 trillion gallons of toxic waste into coastal waters every year.

• A plastic six-pack holder has a life expectancy of 450 years.

DID YOU KNOW? *(cont.)*

Fast Facts

- A three-hour cleanup of 157 miles of Gulf of Mexico shoreline gathered 38,540 plastic lids, 31,773 plastic bags, 30,295 plastic bottles, 15,631 plastic six-pack holders, 7,460 plastic milk jugs, and 1,914 disposable diapers.

- Plastics kill more than a million birds, as well as thousands of seals, sea lions, dolphins, whales, porpoises, and turtles each year.

- In the U.S. we produce over 150 million tons of garbage per year. By the year 2000, that number will be more than 190 million tons.

- Nearly one-third of our current landfills will be full within 5 to 6 years.

- We are currently recycling only about 10% of refuse nationwide.

- Approximately half of all aluminum cans, one third of our newspapers, and one-tenth of our glass bottles are currently recycled.

- Only about 1% of all plastic and very few rubber products, such as tires, are presently recycled.

- Most recycling efforts start with the consumer separating refuse into such elements as metals, glass, paper, and plastic.

- Individual citizens can actively participate in local recycling programs.

- One proposed solution for helping preserve the environment is that local governments plan for collection of and markets for recyclable materials.

- Another proposed solution for environmental preservation is that state governments provide statewide solid waste planning, develop the necessary laws and regulations to enact the plans, and provide for the enforcement of laws and regulations.

- More than 1,000 children in the world die every hour from diarrhea caused by polluted water.

- According to UNICEF estimates, more than 1.4 million children starve to death each year in tropical and subtropical countries. That amounts to 40,000 children per day.

- The production of one ton of paper uses the following resources:
3,688 pounds of wood	76 pounds of soda ash
216 pounds of lime	24,000 gallons of water
360 pounds of salt cake	28 million BTUs of energy

- Producing that one ton of paper creates:
  - 84 pounds of air pollutants
  - 36 pounds of water pollutants
  - 176 pounds of solid waste

9

HOW LONG HAS HUMANKIND BEEN POLLUTING?

Time Chart

Human beings have always polluted the environment. Prior to the Age of Industry and Technology, nature was able to absorb such pollution. In the modern era, however, with the advent and growth of industry and technology, and the increasing demands of an exploding world population, nature has not been able to keep up with or to recover from the burgeoning effects of human pollution. The following chart chronicles key events in the relationship between human society, technology, and the physical environment.

Prehistoric Times — Waste dumped in water. Smoke caused by burning fuel. Pollution was light and spread out over a large area.

Ancient Times — Waste dumped in water. Smoke caused by burning fuel. As people began to dwell in cities, urban pollution problems increased.

500 B.C. — Municipal dump (Athens, Greece).

1647 — Massachusetts Bay Colony passes regulations to prevent the pollution of Boston Harbor.

Late 1700s — Beginning of the Industrial Revolution in England.

1799 — Congress passed the Timber Reservation Act.

1864 — George Perkin Marsh's book *Man and Nature* called attention to environmental issues.

1874 — First incineration of city garbage (Nottingham, England).

1889 — Due to overhunting, the number of buffalo on the American plains dropped from an estimated 60,000,000 to 541.

1890 — New York City street cleaning services began to recycle some wastes.

1899 — Congress passed the River and Harbor Act, making dumping into waterways illegal.

1908 — President Theodore Roosevelt appointed the National Commission for the Conservation of Natural Resources.

1912 — Pollution in the Great Lakes examined by Public Health Service workers.

1913 — Trash-burning plant produced electricity in Milwaukee, Wisconsin.

1935 — Congress created the Soil Conservation Service to control soil erosion.

1936 — The National Wildlife Federation was founded.

1937 — Congress passed the Federal Aid in Wildlife Restoration Act.

1942 — The scarcity of raw materials during World War II led people to increase efforts to recycle.

HOW LONG HAS HUMANKIND BEEN POLLUTING? *(cont.)*

Time Chart

1945 — The first atomic bomb was exploded in New Mexico. Nuclear power was recognized as a source of energy.

1948 — Air pollution from industrial waste and coal-burning furnaces resulted in the deaths of twenty people and caused the illnesses of 14,000.

1956 — Congress passed the Water Pollution Control Act regulating sewage disposal.

1957 — Fire in a plutonium production reactor near Liverpool, England, caused the spread of radioactive material.

1965 — Congress passed an anti-pollution law which mandated automobile emission control measures.

1965 — Congress passed the Solid Waste Disposal Act.

1967 — 37-million-gallon oil spill in Sicily, Italy.

1969 — Major oil spill in Santa Barbara, California.

1969 — The international environmental organization Greenpeace was founded.

1969 — Congress passed the National Environmental Policy Act.

1970 — The first Earth Day was held on April 22.

1970 — Congress passed the Clean Air Act.

1970 — President Nixon established the Environmental Protection Agency (EPA).

1970 — Congress passed the Resource Recovery Act emphasizing recycling.

1971 — 50,000 gallons of radioactive waste water in Monticello, Minnesota, spilled into the Mississippi River.

1972 — Congress passed a pesticide control act banning dichlorodiphenyltrichloroethane (DDT).

1974 — The Worldwatch Institute, which studies global environmental issues, was founded.

1974 — Scientists determined that chlorofluorocarbons (CFCs) can damage the ozone layer of the atmosphere.

1975 — Scientists estimated that one plant or animal species becomes extinct every three days.

1976 — Congress passed the Toxic Substance Control Act prohibiting the use of polychlorinated biphenyls (PCBs).

1976 — Beaches closed due to medical waste washing ashore in New Jersey.

HOW LONG HAS HUMANKIND BEEN POLLUTING? *(cont.)*

Time Chart

1978 — Love Canal region near Niagara Falls, New York, was declared a disaster area because of toxic wastes dumped there.

1978 — 68 million gallons of oil spilled in France.

1979 — Nuclear power plant accident at Three Mile Island, Pennsylvania, contaminated a five-mile area.

1979 — 45 million gallons of oil spilled in Trinidad.

1981 — The Canadian Coalition on Acid Rain worked to promote clean air in Canada and the United States.

1984 — Poisonous gas leak from a pesticide plant in India killed 2,000 people.

1985 — Adopt-A-Highway programs began for highway clean up.

1985 — Scientists determined that from 1945–1985 half the world's rain forests were destroyed.

1986 — Nuclear power plant exploded in Chernobyl, Russia. 31 people died; 200 were injured. Radioactivity detected all over Europe.

1987 — Satellite data confirmed a hole in the Earth's ozone layer over Antarctica.

1988 — East coast beaches closed—waste washed ashore.

1989 — President Bush presented legislation to reduce air pollution by 75% by the year 2000.

1989 — *Exxon Valdez* caused 11-million-gallon oil spill in Alaska. Thousands of animals died.

1990 — President Bush called on Americans to plant one billion trees a year for ten years.

1990 — Eleven oil spills released a total of 14,115,000 gallons of oil into waterways around the world.

1990 — The EPA announced its top priority would be to clean up the Great Lakes.

1990 — Congress revised the Clean Air Act to regulate emissions linked to acid rain.

1991 — April 15, 1991, was declared the first National Recycling Day by Congress.

1991 — Iraq spilled 130 million gallons of oil in the Persian Gulf.

1991 — 650 oil wells in Kuwait were set on fire during the Persian Gulf War, burning more than 11 million gallons of oil and sending tons of smoke and toxic materials into the atmosphere.

WHAT ARE SOME EXAMPLES OF POLLUTION?

Information On Ten Topics

ACID RAIN — A term for the pollution caused when sulfur and nitrogen dioxides combine with rain, hail, dew, snow, or fog.

CAUSES
Coal-fired power plants that burn 100,000,000 tons of coal annually
Smelters
Garbage incinerators
Automobile exhaust (contributes 50% of pollutants)
Fires set to clear land

EFFECTS
Kills fish and shellfish
Causes premature aging of lakes and bays
Destroys animal life
Damages forests and crops
Ruins paint finishes on cars and houses
Corrodes and eats away buildings, monuments, bridges, and highways
Contaminates water supplies
Causes lung disease, asthma, and heart disease

SOLUTIONS
Conserve energy
Use public transportation
Search for alternative forms of transportation
Use stack scrubbers
Recycle
Use non-polluting energy alternatives (wind, solar, renewable)
Enforce efficiency standards for household appliances
Require catalytic converters on all cars worldwide
Support international pollution controls
Burn only low-sulfur oil and coal

WHAT ARE SOME EXAMPLES OF POLLUTION? *(cont.)*

Information On Ten Topics

DESTRUCTION OF RAIN FORESTS — Rain forests are woodlands that receive more than 80 inches of rainfall per year. During the past 30 years, 40% of the rain forests that belt the equator have been destroyed.

CAUSES
Nations struggling with poverty that use rain forests as a way to make money
Rain forests depleted because they are frequently rich sources of:
  Large gold and mineral deposits
  Extensive oil and gas reserves
  A rich supply of hardwood
  Products such as nuts, rubber, oils
Cleared land for ranching and farming
Rain forests depleted because they supply a worldwide demand for lumber to be used for:
  Building construction
  Making furniture
  Plywood and fiberboard
  Charcoal

EFFECTS
Barren land
Broken food chain
Extinct plant and animal life
Polluted atmosphere
Rainwater runoff
Land erosion
Depletion of aquifers
Depletion of disease-treating drug resources
Extinction of native tribes due to disease

SOLUTIONS
Restoration projects
Scientific study
Increased awareness and education
Legislation efforts to protect, conserve, and rehabilitate
Protection as national parks
Reduction of consumption of wood for energy
Promotion of "ecotourism"
International cooperative efforts
Foreign debt forgiveness linked to conservation/preservation
Conservation and recycling of rain forest products

WHAT ARE SOME EXAMPLES OF POLLUTION? *(cont.)*

Information On Ten Topics

ENERGY OVER-CONSUMPTION — Energy consumption is a term used to describe the amount of energy people use in their everyday lives. When the level of energy consumed depletes the earth's resources or pollutes the environment, we call this "energy over-consumption."

CAUSES
Overpopulation
Energy overuse
Energy misuse

EFFECTS
Contributes to pollution problems:
Global warming
Smog
Acid rain
Deforestation
Garbage proliferation
Water pollution
Animal and plant destruction
Human illness and disease

SOLUTIONS
Control amount of energy production
Reduce dependence on fossil fuels
Increase energy efficiency
Promote alternative energy sources: solar, wind, hydro, geothermal
Experiment with new energy sources
Conserve energy
Use renewable energy sources

FRESHWATER POLLUTION — A term used to describe the pollution of our lakes, rivers, springs, streams, groundwater, snow, and ice.

CAUSES
Toxic chemicals discharged either directly into water sources or indirectly
  through leaks
Acid rain
Industrial sludge
By-products of bleaching paper pulp
Thermal pollution
Toxic contamination by pesticides, fertilizers, runoff, de-icing salts

EFFECTS
Pollution of drinking water
Contamination of plants and wildlife
Health problems:
  Hepatitis
  Blindness
  Malaria
  Typhoid
  Cholera
  Leprosy
  Diarrhea
  Cancer
  Birth defects

SOLUTIONS
Sewage treatment
Enforcement of the Clean Water Act of 1972
Water cleanup projects
Reduction of industrial waste
Education aimed at controlling toxic runoff
International cooperation
Chemical recycling to replace dumping
Experimentation with natural pesticides
Legislation
Repair and replacement of inadequate plumbing and sewage systems
Citizen involvement in education and cleanup projects

WHAT ARE SOME EXAMPLES OF POLLUTION? *(cont.)*

Information On Ten Topics

GARBAGE — A term used to describe the trash and waste that is discarded by people.

CAUSES
Cutbacks in "source-separation" programs
Surgence of the throwaway and disposable product
Production of items that cost more to repair than to replace
Failure to recycle reusable materials
Society's failure to invest in saving the environment

EFFECTS
Contamination of drinking water
Air pollution
Costly landfill cleanups

SOLUTIONS
Reduce amount of waste:
  Limit packaging
  Restrict use of disposable products
Reuse products:
  Jars
  Boxes
  Plastic containers
  Furniture
  Clothes
Recycle
Create markets for recycled goods
Compost lawn clippings
Use cloth diapers

WHAT ARE SOME EXAMPLES OF POLLUTION? *(cont.)*
Information On Ten Topics

GLOBAL WARMING — A term used to describe a condition which occurs when the atmosphere traps more heat than normal.

CAUSES
Overpopulation of the planet (currently over 6 billion; expected to double in 60 years)
Increased energy use
Increased automobile emissions
Increased garbage production
Release of chlorofluorocarbons by:
    Refrigerators
    Car air conditioners
    Home insulation
    Fast food containers
Deforestation:
    To provide lumber
    To clear space for building and development
Increased methane production from decomposition:
    Landfills—garbage dumping
    Rice paddies
    Cattle
    Sheep (in New Zealand alone— 900 million gallons yearly)

EFFECTS
Warmer climates
Warmer water temperatures — reducing fish population
Warmer land temperatures — increasing energy demand on air conditioning
Population shift
Business losses
Melting Arctic and Antarctic ice sheets
Raised sea levels:
    Flooding and submerged coastal regions
Salt water intrusion in water supply
Loss of agricultural lands
Shifting rainfall patterns causing deserts to form
Increase in occurrence of violent storms—hurricanes, tornadoes
Changing soil conditions

SOLUTIONS
Slow population growth
Stop deforestation
Develop and use alternative fuel sources:
    Natural gas
    Solar energy
    Wind energy
    Methane gas
    Geothermal
    Hydropower
Increase fuel efficiency/reduce emissions
Recycle refrigerants
Plant trees
Conserve energy/reduce consumption:
    Carpool
    Turn off water
    Turn off appliances when not in use (television, lights, etc.)
Accelerate education and research
Reduce manufacture of chlorofluorocarbons
Convince developing nations to create growth plans that include conservation and efficiency
Seek the cooperation of all nations to find solutions

WHAT ARE SOME EXAMPLES OF POLLUTION? *(cont.)*

Information On Ten Topics

HAZARDOUS WASTE — A term used to identify waste material that is poisonous to plants, animals, the atmosphere, and humans.

CAUSES
Industrial chemicals — 80,000 different kinds
Inappropriate dumping of toxic waste
"Out of sight, out of mind" mentality
Nuclear waste
Inappropriate disposal of household wastes:
    Cleaners
    Insect sprays
    Antifreeze
    Nail polish
    Chlorine bleach
    Paint and solvents

EFFECTS
Contamination of water, air, and ground
Disease
Costs in billions of dollars

SOLUTIONS
Reduction of hazardous waste
Assumption of responsibility:
    Government — to enact and enforce laws
    Industry — to reduce production and clean up waste
    Consumers — to reduce consumption and properly dispose of waste
Detoxification of water
Improvement in the monitoring of waste disposal
Development of scientific experiments and studies to detoxify or separate
    out hazardous waste
Promotion of cleanup campaigns
Establishment of global standards to regulate hazardous waste shipment

Information On Ten Topics

OZONE DEPLETION — A term that describes the reduction of ozone in the Earth's atmosphere. The ozone layer shields the earth from the sun's ultraviolet rays.

CAUSES
Man-made chemicals—chlorofluorocarbons (CFCs)
- Coolants—refrigerators and air conditioners
- Aerosols
- Meat/vegetable/egg trays and cartons
- Fast-food containers
- Foam cushions
- Cleaning agents
- Styrofoam packaging
- Home insulation
- Fire extinguishers

EFFECTS
- Increased incidence of skin cancer
- Increased vulnerability to disease
- Increased incidence of cataracts
- Crop destruction
- Disruption in ocean's food chain
- Mutation of plant and animal organisms
- Climatic changes:
  - Wind patterns
  - Heat in the atmosphere contributes to global warming

SOLUTIONS
- Ban aerosol sprays
- Ban production and use of all CFCs
- Insist on international collaborative efforts
- Recycle CFCs
- Use "natural"cleaning solutions
- Research and develop CFC alternatives
- Create programs for hazardous waste disposal
- Reduce demand for and consumption of CFC materials
- Continue education programs
- Refuse to purchase products that come in polystyrene containers

WHAT ARE SOME EXAMPLES OF POLLUTION? *(cont.)*

Information On Ten Topics

SALT WATER POLLUTION — The term used to describe the pollution of our oceans, seas, gulfs, bays, and inlets.

CAUSES
Much ocean pollution still legal
Sewage
Federally approved sludge dumping grounds
Dumping of toxic chemicals
Plastic throwaways (100 million tons yearly)
Industrial runoff
Oil spills that result from shipping and processing accidents
Overdevelopment of coastal areas

EFFECTS
Closed beaches
Dead marine life
Algae-choked waters
Commercial and recreational fishing jeopardized
Contaminated seafood
Human illnesses — hepatitis

SOLUTIONS
Increased legislation and law enforcement to govern:
    Toxic waste dumping
    Sewage processing and disposal
    Oil drilling and shipment
Reduction of production of waste-producing materials such as plastics
Cleanup campaigns
Control of growth and development along coastlines
Improvement of sewer treatment facilities
Recycling sludge as compost, fertilizer, fuel, and landfill cover
Volunteer watches for polluters
Preventive regulations

WHAT ARE SOME EXAMPLES OF POLLUTION? *(cont.)*

Information On Ten Topics

SMOG — A term for air pollution caused by car exhaust, factory emissions (more than 100 different chemical compounds), dust, ozone, and water droplets.

CAUSES
Car and truck exhaust which contributes 50% of air pollutants
Fires (including home heating fires)
Diesel engines
Leaky gas station pumps
Leaded gas
Cleaning solvents used by dry cleaners
Gas-powered lawn mowers
Barbecue starter fluids
Hair sprays
House paint

EFFECTS
Eye irritation
Lead poisoning
Lung cancer
Chest pains, coughing, scratchy throat
Increase in incidence of infections (colds, pneumonia)
Asthma and emphysema
Slowed fetal growth and development
Brain, nerve, and kidney damage
Destruction of crops and trees

SOLUTIONS
Regulation of smog-producing chemicals
Use of cleaner-burning fuels:
    Ethanol
    Methanol
    Electricity
    Natural gas
    Hydrogen
Enforcement of strict vehicle emission standards
Promotion of car pools and the use of public transportation
Prohibition of gas-powered lawn mowers
Installation of vapor-recovery nozzles at all gas pumps
Cooperation between nations in seeking solutions

WHAT'S IN A HOME?

List Of Biomes

Arctic Tundras *(map below)* .... cold ground with mosses and lichens

Chaparrals *(map on page 24)* .... dry areas with shrubby growth

Deciduous Forests *(map on page 24)* .... trees that shed leaves in winter

Deserts *(map on page 25)* .... arid or semiarid climate

Fresh Water .... inland rivers, lakes, and ponds

Grasslands/Savannahs *(map on page 25)* ....plains with tall grasses

Northern Coniferous Forests *(map on page 26)* .... evergreen trees with cones

Salt Water .... sea life

Tropical Rain Forests *(map on page 26)* .... warm, moist jungles

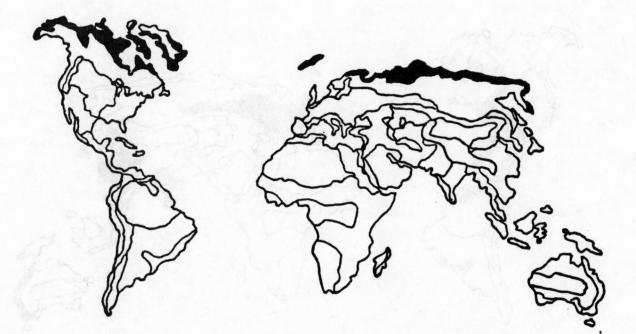

Arctic Tundras

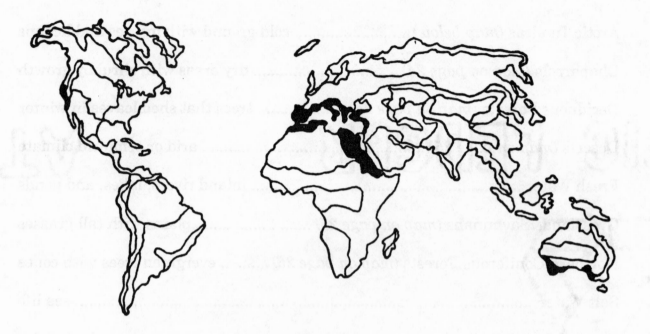

Chaparrals

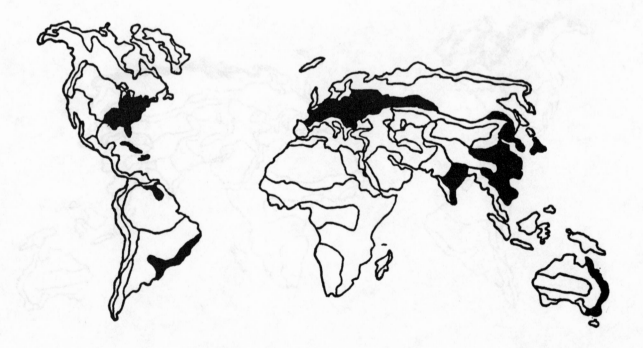

Deciduous Forests

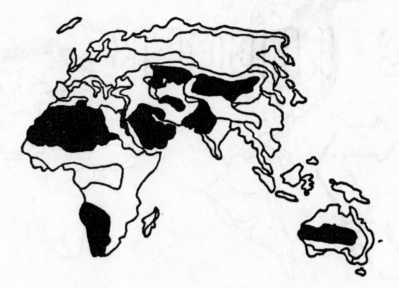

Deserts

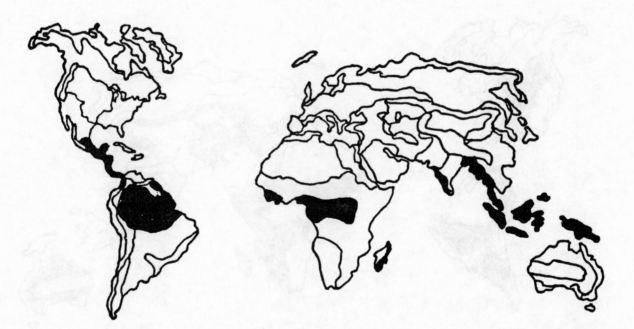

Grasslands / Savannahs

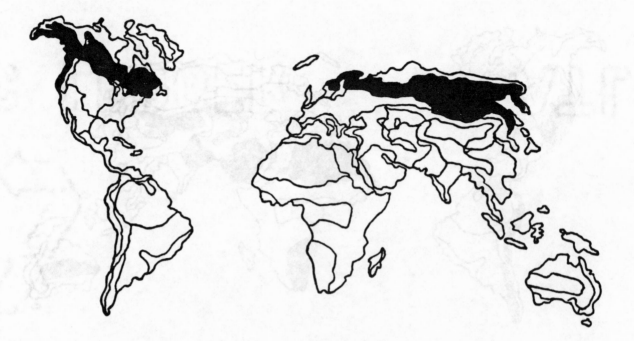

Northern Coniferous Forests

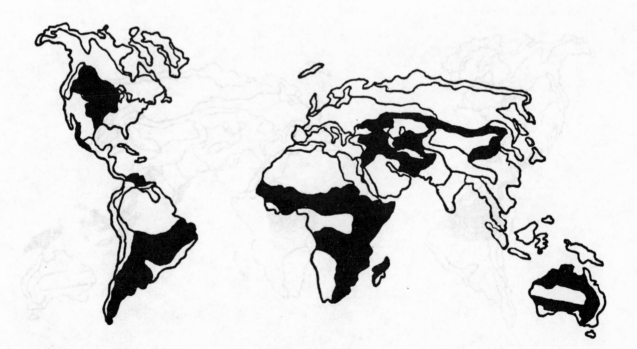

Tropical Rain Forests

WHO LIVES IN JEOPARDY?

Endangered Species

MAMMALS	LOCATION
Asian Wild Ass	Southwestern and Central Asia
Bobcat	Central Mexico
Ozark Big-Eared Bat	United States (MO, OK, AZ)
Brown or Grizzly Bear	United States (48 contiguous states)
Cheetah	Africa to India
Eastern Cougar	Eastern North America
Columbian White-Tailed Deer	United States (WA, OR)
Chinese River Dolphin	China
Asian Elephant	Southcentral and Southeast Asia
San Joaquin Kit Fox	United States (CA)
Gorilla	Central and West Africa
Leopard	Africa, Asia
Asiatic Lion	Turkey to India
Howler Monkey	Mexico to South America
Southeastern Beach Mouse	United States (FL)
Ocelot	United States (TX, AZ)
Southern Sea Otter	United States (WA, OR, CA)
Giant Panda	China
Florida Panther	United States (LA, AR, and east to SC, FL)
Utah Prairie Dog	United States (UT)
Morro Bay Kangaroo Rat	United States (CA)
Black Rhinoceros	Sub-Saharan Africa
Carolina Northern Flying Squirrel	United States (NC, TN)
Tiger	Asia
Hualapai Mexican Vole	United States (AZ)
Gray Whale	North Pacific Ocean
Red Wolf	United States (Southeast to central TX)
Wild Yak	Tibet, India
Mountain Zebra	South Africa

WHO LIVES IN JEOPARDY? *(cont.)*

Endangered Species

BIRDS   LOCATION

Masked Bobwhite (Quail)...................... United States (AZ)

California Condor .... United States (OR, CA)

Hooded Crane .... Japan and CIS (Commonwealth of Independent States)

Eskimo Curlew.. Alaska and North Canada

Bald Eagle .... United States (most states) and Canada

American Peregrine Falcon.................... Canada to Mexico

Hawaiian Hawk .... United States (HI)

Indigo Macaw.. Brazil

West African Ostrich .... Spanish Sahara

Golden Parakeet .... Brazil

Australian Parrot .... Australia

Bachman's Warbler (wood)..................... United States (Southeast) and Cuba

Kirtland's Warbler (wood) .... United States, Canada, and Bahamas

Ivory-Billed Woodpecker .... United States (Southcentral & Southeast) and Cuba

REPTILES

American Alligator .... United States (Southeast)

American Crocodile................................. United States (FL)

Atlantic Salt Marsh Snake.................... United States (FL)

Plymouth Red-Bellied Turtle .... United States (MA)

FISHES

Yaqui Catfish... United States (AZ)

Bonytail Chub .... United States (AZ, CA, CO, NV, UT, WY)

Gila Trout... United States (AZ, NM)

WHO DOESN'T LIVE HERE ANYMORE?

Extinct Species

Extinctions caused by human activities over the last 350 years:

50 species of birds, including:
Dodo (1681)
Great Auk (1844)
Labrador Duck
Moa
Passenger Pigeon (1914)
Carolina Parakeet (1914)

75 species of mammals, including:
Steller's Sea Cow
Guagga (Zebra)
Przewalski's Horse
European Bison
Sea Mink
Merriam Elk

WHAT'S THE CONNECTION?

Food Chain

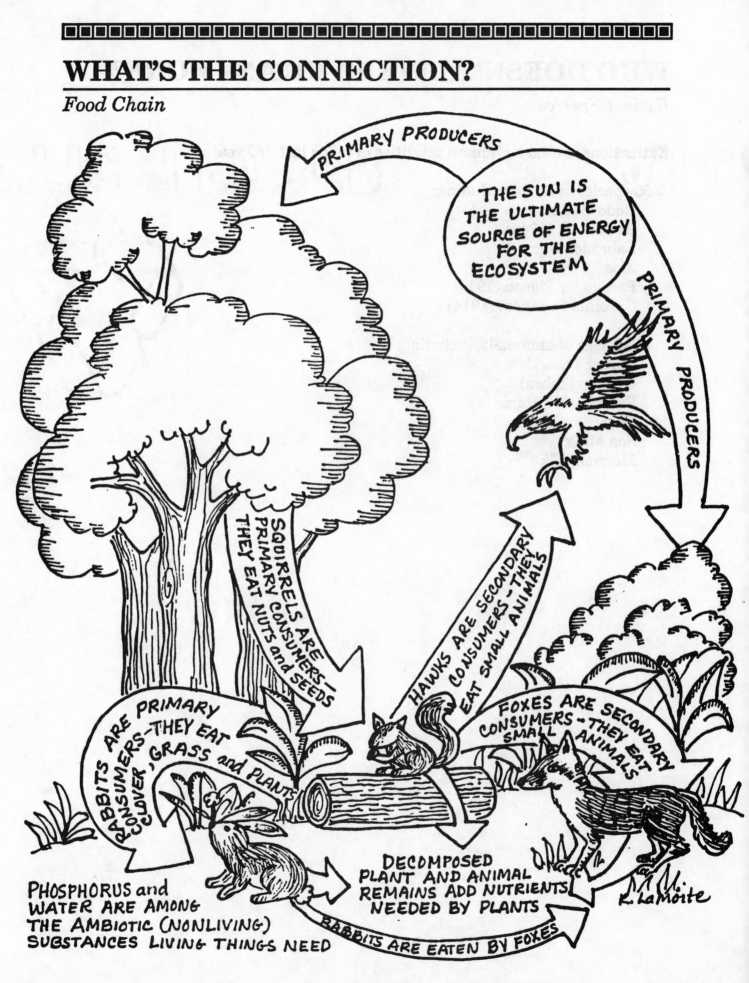

PRIMARY PRODUCERS

THE SUN IS THE ULTIMATE SOURCE OF ENERGY FOR THE ECOSYSTEM

PRIMARY PRODUCERS

SQUIRRELS ARE PRIMARY CONSUMERS— THEY EAT NUTS and SEEDS

HAWKS ARE SECONDARY CONSUMERS—THEY EAT SMALL ANIMALS

FOXES ARE SECONDARY CONSUMERS—THEY EAT SMALL ANIMALS

RABBITS ARE PRIMARY CONSUMERS—THEY EAT CLOVER, GRASS and PLANTS

PHOSPHORUS and WATER ARE AMONG THE AMBIOTIC (NONLIVING) SUBSTANCES LIVING THINGS NEED

DECOMPOSED PLANT AND ANIMAL REMAINS ADD NUTRIENTS NEEDED BY PLANTS

RABBITS ARE EATEN BY FOXES

K. LaMoite

DO YOU KNOW THE DIFFERENCE?

Renew And Recycle And Safely Dispose

Renewable Resources:
  Forests
  Geothermal Energy
  Solar Energy
  Water
  Wildlife
  Wind Energy

Nonrenewable Resources:
  Copper
  Fossil Fuels (coal, oil)
  Lead
  Minerals
  Natural Gas
  Soil
  Zinc

Things That Can Be Recycled:

  Aluminum cans
  Aluminum foil
  Aluminum patio furniture
  Aluminum siding
  Aluminum storm doors
  Aluminum windows
  Automatic transmission fluid
  Battery acid
  Brass
  Cardboard
  Cars
  Computer paper
  Concrete
  Copper
  Diesel fuel
  Dry-cleaning solvents
  Foam polystyrene
  Fuel oil
  Gasoline
  Glass bottles/jars
  Gold
  Gun-cleaning solvents
  Kerosene
  Lawn clippings
  Lead
  Leaves
  Magnetic Metals
  Motor oil
  Newspaper
  Office paper
  Paint brush cleaner with solvent
  Paint thinner
  Paper bags
  Plastic bags (LDPE, HDPE)
  Plastic bottles
  Rags
  Steel
  Tin cans
  Tires
  Turpentine
  Wood
  Zinc

DO YOU KNOW THE DIFFERENCE? *(cont.)*

Renew And Recycle And Safely Dispose

Things That Cannot Be Recycled:
Crystal
Fluorescent bulbs
Light bulbs
Milk-white glass
Nonmagnetic metals
Plastic-coated cellophane
Plate glass
Waxed paper

Hazardous Materials That Need Special Disposal:

Ammunition
Antifreeze
Batteries
Car wax
Diesel fuel
Drain and oven cleaners
Fire extinguishers (old)
Floor care products
Fungicide
Furniture polish
Gasoline
Glue (solvent-based)
Gun cleaning solvent
Herbicide
Insecticide
Kerosene
Lead acid

Lighter fluid
Moth balls
Motor oil
Paint stripper
Paint thinner
Paints (oil-based)
Pesticides
Photographic chemicals
Rat poison
Solvents
Swimming pool chemicals
Transmission fluid
Turpentine
Varnish
Weed killer
Wood preservative

Hazardous Materials Safe to Wash Down the Drain:
Aftershaves, perfumes
Aluminum cleaners
Ammonia-based cleaners
Bathroom cleaners
Disinfectants
Expired medicine
Permanent lotions
Rust remover (with phosphoric acid)
Toilet bowl and drain cleaners
Water-based glue
Window cleaner
Windshield washer solution

IS YOUR HOME HAZARDOUS TO YOUR HEALTH?

PRODUCT TYPE	HAZARDOUS INGREDIENTS	POTENTIAL HAZARDS	ALTERNATIVES / PROPER USE AND DISPOSAL
air fresheners & deodorizers	formaldehyde	toxic; carcinogenic; irritates eyes, nose, throat, and skin; causes damage to nervous, digestive, and respiratory systems	Open a window or use an exhaust fan. Sprinkle baking soda in odor-producing areas or set hot vinegar out in an open dish. Use scented natural potpourri, or boil cinnamon and cloves in water. Use fresh flowers.
bleach *see end note*	sodium hypochlorite	corrosive; irritates and burns skin and eyes; causes damage to nervous, respiratory, and digestive systems	Use a baking soda-and-water cleaning solution.
disinfectants	sodium hypochlorite	corrosive; irritates and burns skin and eyes; causes damage to nervous, respiratory, and digestive systems	Wash items with soap and water or with borax or sodium carbonate (baking soda) in water.
	phenois	ignitable; very toxic; causes damage to respiratory and circulatory systems	
	ammonia	toxic; vapor irritates skin, eyes, and respiratory tract	
drain cleaner	sodium or potassium hydroxide (lye)	corrosive; burns skin, eyes; toxic; causes damage to nervous and digestive systems	Cover drains with screens to prevent clogging. To loosen clogs: Mix 1 cup baking soda, 1 cup salt, and 1 cup white vinegar and pour down drain. Wait 15 minutes. Flush drain with boiling water. Use a rubber plunger or a plumber's snake.
	hydrochloric acid	corrosive; toxic; causes digestive and urinary system damage	
	trichloroethane	toxic; irritates nose and eyes; causes damage to nervous, digestive, and urinary systems	

33

PRODUCT TYPE	HAZARDOUS INGREDIENTS	POTENTIAL HAZARDS	ALTERNATIVES / PROPER USE AND DISPOSAL
flea powder	carbaryl	very toxic; irritates skin; causes damage to nervous, respiratory, circulatory systems	Bathe animals with pet shampoo containing insect-repelling herbs such as rosemary, rue, eucalyptus, and citronella.
	dichlorophene	toxic; irritates skin; causes damage to nervous and digestive systems	
	chlordane, other chlori-nated hydrocarbons	toxic; irritates eyes and skin; causes respira-tory, digestive, and urinary system damage	
floor cleaner/wax	diethylene glycol	toxic; causes nervous, urinary, and digestive system damage	To polish: Mix 1 part thick boiled starch with 1 part soap suds. Rub on floor and polish dry with a clean, soft cloth.
	petroleum solvents	highly ignitable; carcinogenic; irritates skin, eyes, nose, throat, and lungs	To clean: Rub with club soda. Scrub well, let soak, and wipe clean.
	ammonia	toxic; vapor irritates skin, eyes, and respiratory tract	
furniture polish *see end note*	petroleum distillates or mineral spirits	highly ignitable; toxic; carcinogenic; irritates skin, eyes, nose, throat, and lungs	Use olive oil, 100% lemon oil, beeswax, or 2 tsp. lemon oil mixed with 1 pint mineral oil in a spray bottle.
oven cleaner	sodium or potassium hydroxide (lye)	corrosive; burns skin, eyes; toxic; causes damage to nervous and digestive systems	Wipe charred spills with a nonmetallic bristle brush. Scrub baked-on grease & spills with a baking soda, salt, & water solution.
paint thinner	chlorinated aliphatic hydrocarbons	toxic; cause damage to digestive and urinary systems	Use latex paint to eliminate the need for paint thinner.
	esters	toxic; irritate eyes, nose, and throat; cause damage to nervous system	
	alcohols	reactive; ignitable; irritate eyes, nose, & throat	
	chlorinated aromatic hydrocarbons	ignitable; toxic; cause damage to digestive and urinary systems	
	ketones	ignitable; toxic; cause damage to respiratory system	

PRODUCT TYPE	HAZARDOUS INGREDIENTS	POTENTIAL HAZARDS	ALTERNATIVES / PROPER USE AND DISPOSAL
paints	aromatic hydro-carbon thinners	ignitable; toxic; carcinogenic; irritate skin; cause damage to digestive & urinary systems	Use water-based paint and nonaerosol paints.
	mineral spirits	highly ignitable; toxic; irritate skin, eyes, nose, and throat; cause damage to respiratory system	
spot removers	perchlorethylene or trichloroethane	toxic; carcinogenic; causes damage to digestive and urinary systems	Use white vinegar or a solution of equal parts ammonia and water.
	ammonium hydroxide	corrosive; toxic; vapor irritates skin and eyes and causes damage to respiratory system	
	sodium hypochlorite	corrosive; irritates and burns skin and eyes; causes damage to nervous, respiratory, and digestive systems	
toilet bowl cleaner	sodium acid sulfate or oxalate or hypochloric acid	corrosive; toxic; burn skin; cause damage to digestive and respiratory systems	Use 3 Tbs. ammonia, 1 Tbs. white vinegar, and ¾ cup water in a clean spray bottle, or use a solution of 2 Tbs. vinegar in 1 quart water.
	chlorinated phenols	ignitable; very toxic; cause damage to respiratory and circulatory systems	
window cleaners	diethylene glycol	toxic; causes damage to nervous, urinary, and digestive systems	Wipe charred spills with a nonmetallic bristle brush. Scrub baked-on grease and spills with a baking soda, salt, and water solution.
	ammonia	toxic; vapor irritates skin, eyes, and respiratory tract	
antifreeze	ethylene glycol	very toxic; causes damage to circulatory and urinary systems	Antifreeze is toxic and should be disposed of by enclosing in a sealed container and taking to a designated site.
	methanol	toxic; causes damage to nervous and respiratory systems	
carwax/polish	petroleum distillates	toxic; carcinogenic; irritate skin, eyes, and nose; cause damage to respiratory system	Throw away unused portion.

PRODUCT TYPE	HAZARDOUS INGREDIENTS	POTENTIAL HAZARDS	ALTERNATIVES / PROPER USE AND DISPOSAL
wood stains and varnish	mineral spirits, gasoline	highly ignitable; toxic; carcinogenic; irritate skin, eyes, nose, and throat; cause damage to respiratory system	Leftover wood stains and varnish should be enclosed in a sealed container and disposed of in a toxic waste depository.
	methyl and ethyl alcohol	ignitable; toxic; cause nervous system damage	
	benzene	ignitable; toxic; carcinogenic; causes damage to skeletal and digestive system	
	lead	toxic; causes damage to digestive, reproductive, urinary, muscular, and nervous systems	
motor oil	petroleum hydrocarbons, benzene	ignitable; toxic; carcinogenic; irritate skin, eyes, nose, and throat; cause damage to skeletal, digestive, and respiratory systems	Motor oil can be cleaned and recycled. When automobile oil is changed, take it to a service station that will recycle it.
	lead	toxic; causes damage to digestive, reproductive, urinary, muscular, and nervous systems	
herbicides (weed killers)	chlorinated phenoxys (contaminated with dioxin)	toxic; carcinogenic; irritates skin, eyes, and throat	Garden: Spray plants with a solution of 3 Tbs. soap per gallon of water. Spray with purethrum (a chrysanthemum-based natural pesticide).
pesticides	carbamates	toxic; cause damage to nervous system	Household insect spray: Grind 1 clove garlic and 1 onion. Add 1 Tbs. cayenne pepper and 1 quart water. Mix well. Let steep 1 hour. Add 1 Tbs. liquid soap.
	chlorinated hydrocarbons	toxic; carcinogenic; cause damage to nervous system	
	organophosphorus	toxic; causes damage to nervous system	Sprinkle cream of tartar across ants' path. The ants will not cross over.
chemical fertilizers			Compost kitchen and yard wastes in the garden.
detergents (laundry & dishwashing)			Replace detergents with "nontoxic" and biodegradable substitutes.

NOTES

1. Carbamates are marketed under the following names:
   - Aldocarb
   - Oxamy
   - Carbofuran
   - Methyomyl
   - Sectran
   - Propoxur
   - Carbaryl (Sevin)

2. Chlorinated hydrocarbon pesticides are marketed under the following names:
   - Endrin**
   - Aldrin**
   - Dieldrin**
   - Toxaphene**
   - Lindane
   - Benzene**
   - Hexachloride
   - DDT**
   - Heptachlor**
   - Chlordane**
   - Nirex**
   - Methoxychlor

3. Organophosphorus pesticides are marketed under the following names:
   - Phorate
   - Mevinphos*
   - Demeton*
   - Disulfotan
   - Parathoin*
   - Diazinon
   - Trichlorfon
   - Ronnel
   - Azinphosmethy

4. Pesticides marked with a double asterisk (**) are banned or restricted and should NOT be used by households.

* *Not only can many household products be hazardous if used improperly, but they become a danger when improperly disposed of. Improperly-disposed-of chemicals seep into groundwater and eventually reappear in our tap water.*

HOW WASTE-WISE ARE YOU?

Individual Survey

Introduction: Every day people make decisions that affect the amount of waste we produce. Read each item below and circle the number that best describes your behavior.

③ NEVER   ② SOMETIMES   ① OFTEN

1. I avoid eating in carry-out restaurants which package with polystyrene containers.

        3   2   1

2. I think about what will happen to a package or product when I am finished with it.

        3   2   1

3. I avoid using disposable items and batteries when longer-lasting alternatives are available.

        3   2   1

4. I spend money to repair an item even when I can get a new one for close to the same price.

        3   2   1

5. I read consumer articles to learn about the durability and quality of the products I buy.

        3   2   1

6. I consider whether I really need something before purchasing.

        3   2   1

7. I try to reuse things I already have instead of throwing them away and buying new things.

        3   2   1

8. I shop at second-hand stores and/or garage sales.

        3   2   1

HOW WASTE-WISE ARE YOU? *(cont.)*

Individual Survey

9. I write to government officials and leaders to express my concerns about recycling and/or environmental hazards.

        3   2   1

10. I compost kitchen waste and other decomposable organic matter.

        3   2   1

11. When making a buying decision, I consider the pollution and waste that may have been created by a product's manufacture.

        3   2   1

12. I use dishcloths, cloth napkins, and ceramic plates instead of disposable paper products which cannot be recycled.

        3   2   1

13. I take advantage of opportunities to recycle in my area.

        3   2   1

14. I talk to store managers about stocking bulk products to avoid packaging.

        3   2   1

15. I complain to manufacturers about "planned obsolescence."

        3   2   1

Totals = _____ + _____ + _____ Grand total = _____

Note: If your score is 40 or more, you are not considering the environment when you make many decisions.

      A score ranging from 39–21 means you are doing *some* recycling, reducing, and reusing. Find more ways to be "waste-wise."

      If your score is 20 or less, you ARE aware of your environmental decisions and actions. Keep it up.

WHAT CAN I DO?

Personal Actions To Take (For You and Your Parents)

1. Keep your home or car air-conditioning system leak-free. Recycle the refrigerant.

2. Keep refrigerator coils clean and check door seals for damage.

3. When building a new home, choose insulation that does not contain CFCs.

4. Refuse to buy foam cups and plates and products that come in polystyrene containers.

5. Walk, ride a bike or skateboard, or use public transportation whenever possible.

6. Buy beverages packaged in aluminum cans rather than in plastic bottles. Aluminum is more easily recycled.

7. Properly dispose of hazardous waste. Never dump down the drain or on the ground. Call your local waste management office for directions for disposal.

8. Keep the family car tuned up and the spark plugs and oil clean.

9. Avoid buying aerosol sprays. Choose pump sprays, roll-on applicators, and lotions as alternatives.

10. Clean house with "natural" cleaners such as baking powder and vinegar.

11. Use water-based paint instead of oil-based paint when painting your house.

12. Turn off lights and appliances when not in use.

13. Make sure your home fire extinguisher does not use a chemical called Halon 1211, a CFC product.

14. Avoid cigarette smoke, which contains toxic fumes.

15. If you know that a product has been made from a rain forest wood such as teak or mahogany, don't buy it unless you know that the wood was harvested using "tree-sustainable" methods.

16. Support and join environmental groups in order to influence global policies.

WHAT CAN I DO? *(cont.)*

Personal Actions To Take (For You and Your Parents)

17. Write the World Bank and encourage them to include environmental concerns in the planning of every project they initiate: Barber J. Conable, Jr., President, World Bank, 1818 H St., NW, Washington, DC 20433.

18. Plant trees.

19. Help organize and attend rain forest benefits in your community, school, or workplace. Encourage your doctor and local hospital to get involved.

20. Learn what is and is not recyclable, and what products contain recycled goods. Buy recycled goods.

21. Reuse items whenever possible.

22. Encourage source reduction.

23. Precycle. Consider the end result of everything you buy and where it will eventually rest.

24. Compost. Food and yard waste are second to packaging materials in the volume of landfill space they occupy.

25. Pick up at least one piece of trash or litter on the way to and from school and toss it in the nearest trash can.

26. Urge your community to recycle plastic if it does not already do so.

27. Purchase glass bottles rather than plastic containers.

28. Save paper whenever possible. Make double-sided copies when photocopying, reuse paper bags, and use scrap paper for notes.

29. Encourage your local grocery store to carry both paper and plastic recyclable bags. Carry your own string bag to the store.

30. Buy durable products, such as cloth napkins, rather than disposables.

31. When things break, fix them rather than dump them.

32. Organize garage sales to dispose of household goods you no longer use.

33. Don't purchase carbon-zinc batteries. Nickel-cadmium and alkaline batteries last longer, and certain types can be recharged.

WHAT CAN I DO? *(cont.)*

Personal Actions To Take (For You and Your Parents)

34. Speak up. Let your voice and your concerns be heard.

35. Encourage your teachers to reuse household supplies in the classroom.

36. Use this all-purpose cleaner: 1 gal. hot water, ¼ cup sudsy ammonia, ¼ cup vinegar, 1Tbs. baking soda.

37. Don't use nail polish removers that contain formaldehyde resin as a basic ingredient.

38. Use roll-on deodorants instead of aerosol spray deodorants.

39. Don't purchase products packaged with plastic six-pack holders unless the holders are biodegradable. Be sure to cut the holders up before disposing of them.

40. Avoid the use of chemical pesticides or herbicides in your garden.

41. Never dump anything into oceans, gulfs, lakes, bays, etc.

42. Organize beach cleanups on a regular basis.

43. Let your government representatives know how you feel about existing environmental legislation.

44. Conserve water. Consider state-of-the-art toilets and efficient showerheads; check all faucets for leaks; run the dishwasher and washing machine only when full; use phosphate-free, biodegradable dishwashing liquid, laundry detergent, and shampoo.

45. Use natural fertilizers on your garden.

46. Ask lawmakers to mandate strict regulation of ships that carry oil or hazardous waste.

47. Communicate your concern about ocean pollution.

48. Do not flush any type of toxin down toilets or sinks.

49. Purchase organically-grown vegetables and fruits.

50. Use unbleached and undyed paper products whenever possible.

WHAT CAN I DO? *(cont.)*

Personal Actions To Take (For You and Your Parents)

51. Wash your car at home; be sure to turn off the water when you're not using it.

52. Learn about the plants which will grow in your area with little or no watering.

53. Sweep your driveway and sidewalk; do not hose down.

54. If you are concerned about contaminated water, contact: Clean Water Action, 317 Pennsylvania Ave., SE, Washington, DC 20003.

55. Carefully wash and peel fresh fruits and vegetables.

56. When it becomes necessary to replace major appliances in your home, be sure to discover which are most energy-efficient.

57. Use less hot water to save on home heating bills.

58. Save electricity whenever possible.

59. Wrap your hot-water heater with an insulated blanket and lower the temperature to 120 degrees Fahrenheit.

60. Use solar-powered calculators.

61. Do not leave lights and televisions on when you leave your home. Use a timer when away for more than a day.

62. When leaving home for a vacation, turn off pilot lights, water heater, etc.

63. Use fans instead of air conditioners during the summer. During the winter, wear an extra sweater instead of turning up the thermostat.

64. Use a clothesline instead of a clothes dryer.

65. Use shades and curtains to insulate windows; do not cool or heat unused rooms in your home.

66. Help sort school trash into paper, plastic, glass, and aluminum for recycling.

67. Do school assignments on both sides of the paper.

68. Create a conservation bulletin board for your school. Ask all students to contribute.

WHAT CAN WE DO?

Official Actions To Take

1. Substitute abundant resources for those in short supply.

2. Encourage conservation by reducing the amount of waste we produce.

3. Require that engineered landfills be designed to contain liquids that flow through wastes.

4. Encourage nations to work together by sharing technologies and manpower to promote population stabilization programs.

5. Support local planning policies that encourage walking, bicycling, and using mass transit.

6. Encourage strict energy efficiency standards for buildings.

7. Challenge local regulatory commissions to require utilities to promote energy efficiency.

8. Promote a consistent national energy plan.

9. Support government funding for research in alternatives to fossil fuels.

10. Support strict nationwide pollution control measures.

11. Institute programs to collect and safely dispose of household hazardous waste.

12. Promote the use of water conservation devices to reduce water flow to sewage treatment plants.

13. Require strict plans to reduce poison runoff from existing development and to prevent runoff from new development.

14. Encourage each state or locality to implement comprehensive groundwater management laws.

15. Promote incentives and federal support for environmentally sound agricultural practices.

16. Encourage commercial enterprises to find new ways to do business without polluting.

17. Support a nationwide program to collect and safely dispose of household hazardous wastes.

44

WHAT CAN WE DO? *(cont.)*

Official Actions To Take

18. Ban all ocean dumping of medical waste, both directly and through public sewers.

19. Reduce the use of disposable plastics.

20. Encourage uniform labeling so that consumers and businesses know exactly what toxic chemicals are in the products they buy.

21. Encourage government, industry, and environmental groups to work together on source reduction and alternative waste management technology.

22. Advance the adoption of recycling laws in every nation, state, and community.

23. Support higher taxes on nonrecyclable or disposable products.

24. Promote the banning of nondegradable plastics.

25. Require packaging standards for both retail and wholesale products.

26. Encourage developing nations to change economic and other policies that stimulate deforestation and land misuse.

27. Ban the importation of tropical hardwoods.

28. Encourage reforesting by loans, grants, and technical assistance.

29. Support mandatory scrubbers on all coal- and oil-burning power plants and ore smelters.

30. Impose stricter emissions standards for all vehicles.

31. Support the allocation of funding for the research of alternative auto fuels.

32. Back the development of vehicles that use cleaner-burning fuels.

33. Require the installation of controls on gas pumps to capture and recycle vapors which escape during refueling.

34. Enforce the clean air laws already on the books.

35. Issue grants to corporations and businesses that are developing recovery and recycling methods for ozone-depleting substances.

36. Require automobile air conditioner repair locations to recycle refrigerants.

DO YOU WANT SOME TIPS?

Things To Do

How To Prepare Materials for Recycling:

Glass: Rinse and separate by color (clear, green, brown). Store unbroken.

Plastics: Rinse, flatten, and store soft drink and detergent bottles, milk jugs, etc.

Motor Oil: Drain carefully and store in a clean, sealed container.

Metals: Rinse, flatten, and store aluminum and tin cans.

Paper: Stack and bundle (tie or put in paper bags).

Corrugated Cardboard: Remove staples and tape. Flatten, stack, and bundle.

Ways To Make Recycling a Success:

1. Share your enthusiasm for recycling with family, neighbors, and friends.

2. Encourage local officials to institute recycling programs in your community.

3. Buy recycled goods: paper, bottles, cans, etc.

4. Choose durable (reusable) goods such as rechargeable batteries, cloth diapers, and dishes.

5. Limit purchases — borrow and rent things; patronize libraries and used book stores.

6. Sell or donate leftovers: unwanted paint, outgrown clothing, furniture, and appliances. Have a garage sale.

7. Avoid hazardous chemicals. Read product labels carefully. Choose nonhazardous materials whenever possible. Dispose of chemicals only as directed.

8. Start a compost pile. Recycle vegetable peels, lawn clippings, etc.

DO YOU WANT SOME TIPS? *(cont.)*

Things To Do

Become an Activist: Write Letters

Use this checklist before and after you write your letter.

___ Be brief, concise, polite; address a single issue.

___ Include your full name, home address, and telephone number.

___ Explain your reasons for writing. Describe environment-threatening situations which could affect you and your neighborhood.

___ Express your own views.

___ Double-check the name and address of the official to whom you are writing.

___ Begin with a clear statement of your concern. If this involves legislation, be sure to include the bill number or a full description.

___ Include published facts and figures that support your view.

___ Request a written response.

___ End the letter on a positive note. Thank the official for his or her time and attention to the matter.

WHO SAID THAT?

Quotations

"If you don't buy recycled products, you're not recycling."
Will Steger

"Think globally, act locally."
Buckminster Fuller

"Until we commit to cleaning up our personal act, all the high-tech fixes and international forums won't make a difference. . . . The 40% destruction of the equator's tropical rain forests is the greatest extinction since the end of the dinosaurs."
E. O. Wilson

"Waste is a tax on the whole people."
Albert W. Atwood

"A nation's growth from sea to sea
Stirs in his heart who plants a tree."
H. C. Bunner

"Living in the midst of abundance we have the greatest difficulty in seeing that the supply of natural wealth is limited and that the constant increase of population is destined to reduce the American standard of living unless we deal more sanely with our resources."
W. H. Carothers

"Trouble always follows the destruction of the forests on the headwaters of the streams."
Harold W. Fairbanks

"Conservation does not mean the locking up of our resources, nor a hindrance to real progress in any direction. It means only wise, careful use."
Mary Huston Gregory

"Our wild-life resources are among our most valuable assets, and there can be no higher public duty than to aid in their preservation."
Charles Lathrop Pack

"This nation must make both ends meet by living within its means. That calls for wasting less and producing more—for growing bigger crops, for so handling the forests as to improve them, for common sense and knowledge and self-restraint in our use, not only of what grows, but of the things which do not grow, like minerals and water. Today we are not living within our means. Until we do we are harming ourselves, and we are robbing those who will come after us."
Overton W. Price

WHO SAID THAT? *(cont.)*

Quotations

"The conservation of our natural resources and their proper use constitute the fundamental problem which underlies almost every other problem of our national life."
   Theodore Roosevelt

"Of all the sinful wasters of man's inheritance on earth, and all are in this regard sinners, the very worst are the people of America."
   Nathaniel Southgate Shaler

"Stop killing and start creating. Stop cutting and start planting. Stop wasting and start saving. Stop hating and start loving. These are the ten commandments of conservation for each of us within his own dooryard and neighborhood, over his own ranch and farm; a sower of seed, a planter of trees, a nourisher of life, where heretofore we have each plucked and burned and slaughtered."
   Dallas Lore Sharp

"Conservation, while a question of national importance, is at bottom a local issue. . . . With government, so with conservation; to be for the people, conservation must be by the people."
   George Otis Smith

"Conservation means 'the greatest good to the greatest number—and that for the longest time'."
   Charles Richard Van Hise

"The lengthening of human life is ultimately connected with that of the conservation of the natural resources."
   Charles Richard Van Hise

"Anything that is irreplaceable should be conserved and protected for its fullest use."
   Ray Lyman Wilbur and William Atherton DuPay

WHO SAID THAT? *(cont.)*

Quotations

The following quotations are anonymous.

"Our actions are our own; their consequences are not."

"Freedom is a package deal—with it comes responsibilities and consequences."

"Good intentions die unless they are executed."

"You can't clean up this old world with soft soap; it takes grit."

"Think right, act right; it is what you think and do that makes you what you are."

"We make our future by the best use of the present."

"Do it now! Today will be yesterday tomorrow."

"It is not enough to make progress; we must make it in the right direction."

WHERE CAN YOU GET MORE INFORMATION?

Resources

I. ARTICLES

Browne, Malcolm W. "New Tactics Emerge in Struggle Against Smog." *The New York Times,* February 21, 1989.

"Buried Alive," *Newsweek*, November 27, 1990, page 66.

Christup, Judy. "Clamping Down on International Waste Trade." *Greenpeace*, November/December 1988.

"A Citizen's Handbook on Water Quality Standards," Natural Resources Defense Council Clean Water Project, 1350 New York Ave., NW, Suite 300, Washington, DC 20005.

Cobb, Charles E., Jr. "The Great Lakes' Troubled Waters." *National Geographic*, July 1987

"Crisis in the Rain Forests," *Mother Earth News*, July/August 1987.

Doniger, David. "Politics of the Ozone Layer." *Issues of Science and Technology*, Vol. 4, No. 3, 1988.

Ellis, William S. "Brazil's Imperiled Rain Forest." *National Geographic*, December 1988.

Frumkin, Paul. "Trash Clash." *Restaurant Business*, May 20, 1989.

"Hazardous Waste from Homes," Enterprise for Education, 1320-A Santa Monica Mall, Suite 202, Santa Monica, CA 90401.

Heise, Lori and Sandra Postel. "Deforesting the Earth." *State of the World,* The Worldwatch Institute, 1988.

"Intolerable Risk: Pesticides in Our Children's Food," report by the Natural Resources Defense Council, February 1989.

Kunes, Ellen. "The Trashing of America." *Omni*, February 1988.

Luoma, Jon R. "Acid Murder No Longer a Mystery." *Audubon*, November 1988.

_____. "Trash Can Realities." *Audubon*, March 1990, page 86.

Oates, Thomas L. and Kevin W. Thorpe, Ph.D. "Finding Safe Alternatives to Pesticides." *Clean Water Action News*, Winter 1989.

Resources

Page, Jake. "Clear-Cutting the Tropical Rain Forest in a Bold Attempt to Salvage It." *Smithsonian*, April 1988.

Porter, J. Winston. "Our Garbage Problem Won't Go Away by Itself." *Chemeology*, September 1989, Vol. 18, No. 7, pages 2–4.

Praded, Joni, ed. "Oceans at Risk: Animals Face the Challenge of a Troubled Sea." *Animals*, January/February 1989.

Schindler, D. W. "Effects of Acid Rain on Freshwater Ecosystems." *Science*, Vol. 239, January 8, 1988.

Shoumatoff, Alex. "Murder in the Rain Forest." *Vanity Fair*, April 1989.

Skolnick, Racquel. "Persistent and Poisonous. What Does it Take to get a Toxic Chemical off the Market?" *Greenpeace*, Vol. 12, No. 1.

"Stepping Lightly on the Earth: Everyone's Guide to Toxics in the Home." Greenpeace Action, 1436 U St., NW, Suite 201-A, Washington, DC 20009.

"U.S. Water News" (monthly), U.S. Water News Circulation Dept., 230 Main St., Halstead, KS 67056

Weisman, Alan. "L. A. Fights for Breath." *The New York Times Magazine*, July 30, 1989.

Weisskopf, Michael. "Plastic Reaps a Grim Harvest in Oceans of the World." *Smithsonian*, March 1988.

Williams, Ted. "The Metamorphosis of Keep America Beautiful." *Audubon*, March 1990, page 124.

Wolkonur, Richard. "I Learned That It Just Keeps Getting Deeper." *Smithsonian*, April 1990, Vol. 21, No. 1, page 147.

WHERE CAN YOU GET MORE INFORMATION? *(cont.)*

Resources

II. BOOKS AND JOURNALS

Ashworth, William. *The Late, Great Lakes.* New York: Summit Books, 1982.

Beyea, Jan. *Audubon Energy Plan.* National Audubon Society, 950 Third Ave., New York, NY 10022.

Biocycle. The JG Press, Inc., Box 351, 18 S. 7th St., Emmaus, Pennsylvania 18049.

Bulloch, David K. *The Wasted Ocean.* New York: Lyons and Burnford, 1989.

A Citizen's Guide to Plastics in the Ocean: More Than a Litter Problem. Center for Marine Conservation, 1725 DeSales St., NW, Suite 500, Washington, DC 20036.

Coffel, Steve. *But Not a Drop to Drink: The Lifesaving Guide to Good Water.* Rawson & Associates, New York: Macmillan, 1989.

Drinking Water: A Community Action Guide. Concern, 1794 Columbia Rd., NW, Washington, DC 20009.

Duvail, Carol. *Wanna Make Something Of It?* Nash Publishing, Los Angeles, California.

Ehrlich, Paul. *The Population Explosion.* New York: Ballantine, 1990.

Energy for a Sustainable World. The World Resources Institute, 1709 New York Ave. NW, Washington, DC 20006.

Fact Sheet on Acid Rain. Canadian Embassy Public Affairs Division, 1771 N Street, NW, Washington, DC 20036-2879.

Fornos, Werner. *Gaining People, Losing Ground: A Blueprint for Stabilizing World Population.* The Population Institute, Washington, DC, 1987.

Girardet, Herbert and John Seymour. *Blueprint for a Green Planet: Your Practical Guide to Restoring the World's Environment.* New York: Prentice-Hall, 1987.

The Good Wood Guide. Friends of the Earth, London, 1988.

Hassol, Susan and Beth richman.*Energy: 101 Practical Tips for Home and Work..* Snowmass, CO: The Windstar Foundation, 1989.

_____. *Everyday Chemicals: 101 Practical Tips for Home and Work.* Snowmass, CO: The Windstar Foundation, 1989.

_____. *Recycling: 101 Practical Tips for Home and Work.* Snowmass, CO: The Windstar Foundation, 1989.

Head, Susan, ed. *Lessons From the Rain Forest.* San Francisco: Sierra Club Books, 1990.

How To Recycle Waste Paper. American Paper Institute, 260 Madison Ave., New York, NY 10017.

Resources

Kane, Joe. *Running the Amazon.* New York: Knopf, 1989.

Kirshner, Dan and Adam C. Stern. *To Burn or Not to Burn.* Environmental Defense Fund, 257 Park Ave. South, New York, NY 10010.

Lowe, Marcia D. *The Bicycle: Vehicle for a Small Planet.* Washington, DC: Worldwatch Institute, 1989.

MacEachern, Diane. *Save Our Planet—750 Everyday Ways You Can Help Clean Up the Earth.* 1990. Dell Publishing, 666 Fifth Ave., New York, NY 10103.

Mason Hunter, Linda. *The Healthy Home: An Attic-To-Basement Guide to Toxin-Free Living.* Rodale Press, 1989.

McKibben, Bill. *The End of Nature.* New York: Random House, 1989.

Palmer, Tim. *Endangered Rivers and the Conservation Movement.* Berkeley and Los Angeles: University of California Press, 1986.

Pollock Shea, Cynthia. *Protecting Life on Earth: Steps to Save the Ozone Layer.* Worldwatch Paper 87, Worldwatch Inst.

Price, David. *Before the Bulldozer: The Nambiquara Indians and the World Bank.* Seven Locks Press, 1989.

Pringle, Laurence. *Throwing Things Away: From Middens to Resource Recovery.* 1986. Thomas Y. Crowell, 10 East 53 Street, New York, NY 10022.

Recycling Today. Gie, Inc., Publishers, 4012 Bridge Ave., Cleveland, Ohio 44113.

Resource Recovery and the Environment. National Solid Waste Management Assoc., 1730 Rhode Island Ave., NW, Washington, DC 20036.

Resource Recycling. 1615 N.W. 23rd, Suite 1, P.O. Box 10540, Portland, Oregon 97210.

Saving the Ozone Layer: A Citizen's Action Guide. New York: Natural Resources Defense Council, 1989.

Schneider, Stephen. *Global Warming: Are We Entering the Greenhouse Century?* San Francisco: Sierra Club Books, 1989.

USA by Numbers. (Tracks trends from acid rain to zero population growth, for kids and adults.) Zero Population Growth, 1400 16th St., NW, Suite 320, Washington, DC 20036.

Waste Age Recycling Times. 5616 West Cermack Rd., Cicero, Illinois 60650.

Waste Reduction: The Only Serious Waste Reduction Management Option. Citizens Clearinghouse for Hazardous Waste, Box 926, Arlington, VA 22216.

Water Rights: Scarce Resource, Allocation, Bureaucracy, and the Environment. Pacific Institute for Public Policy Research, 177 Post St., San Francisco, CA 94108.

WHERE CAN YOU GET MORE INFORMATION? *(cont.)*

Resources

III. CURRICULUM FOCUS

A-Way With Waste: A Waste Management Curriculum for Schools (K-12), 1984. Washington State Department of Ecology, Litter Control and Recycling Program, 4250-150th Ave., NE, Redmond, WA 98052.

Class Project: Conservation Learning Activities for Science and Social Studies. National Wildlife Federation, 1412-16th St., NW, Washington, DC 20036.

Dodge County Says Please Recycle. 15-min. slide-tape. Dodge Co. Library Service, 311 N. Spring St., Juneau, WI 53039.

Energy Where You Least Expect It. 28-min. film. Third Eye Films, 12 Arrow St., Cambridge, MA 02138.

A Guide to Curriculum Planning in Environmental Education. David C. Engleson, 1985. Wisconsin Department of Public Instruction, P. O. Box 7841, Madison, WI 53705-5841.

Ohio Science Workbook: Litter Prevention and Recycling, 1987. The Ohio Academy of Science, 445 King Avenue, Columbus, Ohio 43201.

Ranger Rick: Recycling Reprints. National Wildlife Federation, 1412 16th St., NW, Washington, DC 20036.

Recycle America. 8-min. VHS video. Waste Management Inc., 3963 N. Federal Hwy., Fort Lauderdale, FL 33308.

Recycling Lesson Plans (K-12). Pennsylvania Department of Environmental Resources, Bureau of Waste Management, Recycling and Waste Reduction, P. O. Box 2063, Harrisburg, PA 17120.

Recycling. 9-min. VHS video. Recycling Advisory Committee, 119 King Street West, Hamilton, Ontario L8N3Z9.

Reduction, Reuse, Recycling (K–12). Association of Oregon Recyclers, 1615 NW 23rd Ave., Suite 1, Portland, OR 97210.

Super Savers Investigators K–8 Curriculum Guide. Ohio Department of Natural Resources, Division of Litter Prevention and Recycling, Fountain Square, Bldg. F-2, Columbus, OH 43224.

Toxics in My Home? You Bet! K-3 and 4-6 Curriculum Guides. Golden Empire Health Planning Center, Sacramento, CA.

Waste In Place. K–6 Curriculum Guide. Keep America Beautiful, Inc., Mill River Plaza, 9 West Broad St., Stanford, CT 06902.

WHERE CAN YOU GET MORE INFORMATION? *(cont.)*

Resources

IV. ORGANIZATIONS/AGENCIES

Acid Rain Information Clearinghouse Library, Center for Environmental Information, Inc., 33 S. Washington St., Rochester, NY 14608.

Alliance to Save Energy, 1925 K St., NW, Suite 206, Washington, DC 20036.

Aluminum Association Inc., 900 19th St., NW, #300, Washington, DC 20006.

American Forestry Association, 1516 P Street, NW, Washington, DC 20005.

American Paper Institute, 260 Madison Ave., New York, NY 10016.

American Wilderness Alliance, 6700 East Arapahoe, Suite 114, Englewood, CO 80112.

Can Manufacturers Institute, 1625 Massachusetts Ave., NW, Washington, DC 20036.

Center for Plastics Recycling Research, Rutgers University, Building 3529-Busch Campus, Piscataway, NJ 08855.

Clean Water Action, 733 15th St., NW, Suite 1110, Washington, DC 20005.

Defenders of Wildlife, 1244 19th St., NW, Washington, DC 20036.

Department of the Interior, U.S. Fish and Wildlife Service, National Ecology Center, Leetown, Box 705, Kearneysville, WV 25430.

Edison Electric Institute, 1111 19th St., NW, Washington, DC 20036.

Environmental Defense Fund, 257 Park Avenue South, New York, NY 10010.

Friends of the Earth, 530 7th St., SE, Washington, DC 20003.

Glass Packaging Institute, 1801 K St., NW, #1105-L, Washington, DC 20006.

Greenpeace USA, 1436 U St., NW, Washington, DC 20009.

WHERE CAN YOU GET MORE INFORMATION? *(cont.)*

Resources

INFORM, 381 Park Ave., South, New York, NY 10017.

Institute of Scrap Recycling Industries, 1627 K Street, NW, #700, Washington, DC 20006

Keep America Beautiful, Inc., 99 Park Ave., New York, NY 10022.

National Association for Plastic Container Recovery, 4828 Parkway Plaza Blvd., #260, Charlotte, NC 28217.

National Audubon Society, 801 Pennsylvania Ave., SE, Suite 301, Washington, DC 20003.

National Clean Air Coalition, 530 7th St., SE, Washington, DC 20003.

National Recycling Coalition, 1101 30th St., NW, #305, Washington, DC 20007.

National Soft Drink Association, 1101 16th St., NW, Washington, DC 20036.

National Solid Waste Management Association, 1120 Connecticut Ave., NW, Washington, DC 20005.

National Wildlife Federation, 1412 16th St., NW, Washington, DC 20036.

Nuclear Information and Resource Service, 1424 16th St., NW, Suite 601, Washington, DC 20036.

Rain Forest Action Network, 301 Broadway, Suite A, San Francisco, CA 94133.

Renew America, 1400 16th St., NW, Suite 710, Washington, DC 20036.

Resources for the Future, 1616 P St., NW, Washington, DC 20036.

Sierra Club, 730 Polk St., San Francisco, CA 94109.

Student Conservation Association, Inc., P. O. Box 550, Charlestown, NH 03630.

The Cousteau Society, 930 W. 21st St., Norfolk, VA 23517.

WHERE CAN YOU GET MORE INFORMATION? *(cont.)*

Resources

The Nature Conservancy, 1815 N. Lynn St., Arlington, VA 22209.

U.S. Council for Energy Awareness, P. O. Box 66103, Dept. AY31, Washington, DC 20035.

U.S. Environmental Protection Agency, 401 M St., SW, Washington, DC 20460.

United Nations Population Fund, 220 E. 42nd St., New York, NY 10017.

Water Pollution Control Federation, Education Department, 601 Wythe St., Alexandria, VA 22314-1994.

Wildlife Conservation International, New York Zoological Society, Bronx, NY 10460-9973.

World Society for the Protection of Animals, 29 Perkins Street, P. O. Box 190, Boston, MA 02130.

World Wildlife Fund, 1250 24th St., NW, Washington, DC 20037.

Worldwatch Institute, 1776 Massachusetts Ave., NW, Washington, DC 20036.

Zero Population Growth, 1400 16th St., NW, Suite 320 Washington, DC 20036.

GLOSSARY

abiotic substances – substances, such as water and phosphorous, that are necessary to sustain life

acid rain – rain which contains acid caused by air pollution; destroys forests and bodies of water and damages crops

air pollution – harmful substances deposited in the air that cause a dirty, unhealthy, or hazardous condition

alternatives – other possible ways of dealing with, treating, or disposing of wastes or of producing energy

aquifer – an underground water source, usually a river or seepage, that provides water for human and animal use from wells or springs

ash – the solid residue left when combustible material is thoroughly burned or is oxidized by chemical means

biodegradable – a substance or material that can be broken down into simpler compounds by microorganisms and other decomposers such as fungi

bulk products – products packaged in large quantities

chlorofluorocarbons (CFCs) – any of a group of chemicals that contains chlorine, fluorine, and carbon; often used as refrigerants and cleaning solvents. When released into the air, CFCs destroy the ozone layer that protects the earth.

chronic exposure – receipt of a small dose of a hazardous substance over a long period of time

climate – the weather conditions of a particular place

compost – the product of composting; a mixture that consists largely of decayed organic matter used to improve soil

composting – a waste management alternative in which organic wastes are partially decomposed by aerobic bacteria and fungi to produce a material that enriches the soil

conservation – the use of natural resources in a way that assures they will be available for future generations

consumption – the amount of any resource (material or energy) used in a given time

decompose – to separate into constituent parts or elements or into simpler compounds; to undergo chemical breakdown; to decay or rot as a result of microbial and fungal action

decomposers – bacteria and fungi which break down dead plants and animals into simple nutrients

decomposition – the act of undergoing breakdown into constituent parts

deforestation – the clearing of forest land

degradable – capable of being broken down into smaller components by chemical, physical, or biological means

detoxify – to remove the poisonous substance from a material

GLOSSARY

direct energy cost – the energy used to manufacture a product

disposable – something that is designed to be used once and then thrown away

disposal – the process by which something is gotten rid of or thrown away

dump – a site where mixed wastes are indiscriminately deposited, without controls or regard to the protection of the environment

ecologist – a person who studies the interrelationships of organisms and their environment

ecosystem – a community of plants and animals and the environment with which it is interrelated

ecotourism – a source of income received when tourists pay to see pristine ecosystems such as the rain forest. It provides income to the area and, if properly managed, saves the environment.

energy – ability to do work by moving matter or by causing a transfer of heat between two objects at different temperatures

environment – the total of all our surroundings—air, water, land, people, and animals—which influence how we live

EPA – (U.S. Environmental Protection Agency) the federal agency charged with the enforcement of all federal regulations having to do with air and water pollution, radiation and pesticide hazard, ecological research, and solid waste disposal

ethanol – a clean fuel substitute for gasoline that is made from corn

finite – having limits or being limited; not endless in quantity or duration

garbage – refuse consisting of food wastes; animal and vegetable wastes resulting from the handling, storage, sale, preparation, cooking, and serving of foods

global warming – a condition which occurs when the atmosphere begins to trap more heat than normal; caused by pollution

greenhouse effect – a condition in which the earth's atmosphere traps heat in the same way as greenhouse glass

groundwater – water stored in the porous spaces of underground soil and rock

habitat – a place or type of place where an organism or community of organisms lives and thrives; contains food, water, shelter, and space

hazardous waste – anything thrown away that is harmful to human beings and the environment

hydroelectric power – the electricity produced by water power

incinerator – a facility designed to control the burning of waste; reduces waste volume by converting waste into gases and relatively small amounts of ash; may offer potential for energy recovery

indirect energy – energy that is used to make and move products but is not directly involved in the production process

landfill – location where garbage and trash are disposed of by burying and covering with soil

GLOSSARY

leaching – the process by which water infiltrating through the soil which covers a landfill percolates down through the waste and picks up suspended and dissolved materials from the waste

litter – highly visible solid waste that is generated by consumers and is carelessly and/or improperly discarded

methane – a colorless, odorless, flammable, and potentially dangerous gaseous hydrocarbon present in natural gas and formed by the decomposition of organic matter; can be used as a fuel

methanol – a clean fuel alternative substitute for gasoline made from coal or natural gas

municipal – having to do with the government of a city or town

natural gas – a mixture of gaseous hydrocarbons, chiefly methane, used as fuel

nonrecyclable – not capable of being recycled or used again

nonrenewable (resource) – not capable of being naturally restored or replenished; resources available in a fixed amount (stock) in the earth's crust; they can be exhausted either because they are not replaced by natural processes or because they are replaced more slowly than they are consumed

nuclear waste – radioactive waste from a nuclear power plant

organic – composed of living or once-living matter; more broadly, containing chemical compounds principally composed of the element carbon, excluding carbon dioxide

ozone depletion – the partial destruction of the earth's ozone layer by CFCs and other pollutants. The gaseous ozone layer protects the earth from the sun's harmful ultraviolet rays.

packaging – the materials used to wrap, contain, and protect products

pesticide – any chemical used to control the growth of plants and animals; often harmful to people

planned obsolescence – the practice of producing goods that have a very short lifespan so that more goods will have to be produced

pollute – to contaminate; to make impure

pollution – harmful substances deposited in the air, water, or land that cause a dirty, unhealthy, or hazardous condition

primary consumers – plant-eating animals

primary producers – green plants that make food through the process of photosynthesis

radioactive – a substance capable of giving off high-energy particles or rays as a result of spontaneous disintegration of atomic nuclei

rain forest (tropical) – a tropical woodland with over 100 inches of annual rainfall and marked by lofty broadleafed trees that form a canopy; usually found near the Equator

GLOSSARY

recycle – to separate a given material from waste and process it so that it can be used again in a form similar to its original use; for example, newspapers are recycled into newspapers or cardboard

renewable (resource) – capable of being naturally restored or replenished; a resource capable of being replaced by natural ecological cycles or sound management practices

resource – a natural or man-made material that can be used to make something else; for example, wood resources are made into paper and old bottles can be made into new ones

reuse – finding new functions for objects and materials that have outgrown their original use; to use again

runoff – water that flows across the surface of the ground—rather than soaking into it—eventually entering bodies of water; may pick up and carry with it a variety of suspended or dissolved substances

secondary consumers – animal-eating predators

sewage – liquid and solid human wastes carried off with water in sewers and drains

sludge – solid matter that settles to the bottom of septic tanks or waste-water treatment plant sedimentation tanks; must be processed by bacterial digestion or other methods, or pumped out for land disposal, incineration, or composting

smog – air pollution that engulfs most large cities; caused primarily by car exhaust and factory emissions

solar energy – the power produced by the sun's energy

solid waste – any of a wide variety of solid materials which are discarded or rejected as being spoiled, useless, worthless, or in excess; includes garbage, refuse, yard trash, clean debris, white goods, special waste, ashes, sludge, or other discarded material

source separation – the separating of recyclable materials from waste at the place of use

thermal pollution – warm water that, when returned to its source after cooling power plant generators, takes oxygen out of water, disrupting and killing plant and animal life

toxic waste – poisonous, dangerous, and often lethal waste; similar to hazardous waste

urban population – people living in a city and nearby area in which the total population numbers more than 50,000 people

virgin (materials) – term describing raw materials as yet unused; for example, virgin aluminum has not yet been fabricated into cans

waste – anything that is discarded, useless, or unwanted

wind power – the power produced by wind energy

MORE TOPICS TO INVESTIGATE

- ACID RAIN
- AIR POLLUTION
- CARBON DIOXIDE
- CONSERVATION
- CHLOROFLUOROCARBONS (CFCs)
- DEFORESTATION
- ECOLOGY
- ENDANGERED SPECIES
- ENERGY EFFICIENT AUTOMOBILES
- ENERGY EFFICIENT HOMES
- ENVIRONMENTAL POLLUTION
- FOOD CHAIN/LIFE CYCLE
- GARBAGE DUMPING
- GLOBAL WARMING
- GREENHOUSE EFFECT
- HAZARDOUS WASTE
- INCINERATION
- OVERPOPULATION
- OZONE DEPLETION
- POPULATION DYNAMICS
- RAIN FORESTS
- RECYCLING (motor oil, tires, aluminum, paper, glass)
- SALT WATER
- SMOG
- SOLAR ENERGY
- TEMPERATURE INVERSION
- THERMAL POLLUTION
- TOXIC WASTE
- TRASH-TO-ENERGY CONVERSION
- WASTE MANAGEMENT